STICKMEN'S GUIDE
TO
MATH

Thanks to the creative team:
Senior Editor: Alice Peebles
Fact Checking: Tim Harris
Design: Perfect Bound Ltd

Hungry Tomato®
A division of Lerner Publishing Group, Inc.
241 First Avenue North
Minneapolis, MN 55401 USA

For reading levels and more information, look up
this title at www.lernerbooks.com.

Main body text set in Avenir LT Std 9/5/12.
Typeface provided by Linotype AG.

Library of Congress Cataloging-in-Publication Data

Names: Farndon, John, author. | Matthews, Joe,
1963– illustrator.
Title: Stickmen's guide to math / John Farndon ; Joe
Matthews [illustrator].
Description: Minneapolis : Hungry Tomato, [2018] |
Series: Stickmen's guide to STEM | Audience: Ages
8-12. | Audience: Grades 4 to 6.
Identifiers: LCCN 2018010791 (print) | LCCN
2018016434 (ebook) | ISBN 9781541523968 (eb pdf)
| ISBN 9781541500624 (lb : alk. paper)
Subjects: LCSH: Mathematics—Juvenile literature. |
Mathematics—History—Juvenile literature.
Classification: LCC QA141.3 (ebook) | LCC QA141.3
.F37 2018 (print) | DDC 510—dc23

LC record available at https://lccn.loc.
gov/2018010791

Manufactured in the United States of America
1-43707-33495-4/19/2018

STICKMEN'S GUIDE

TO

MATH

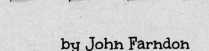

by John Farndon

Illustrated by Joe Matthews

HUNGRY TOMATO®

Minneapolis

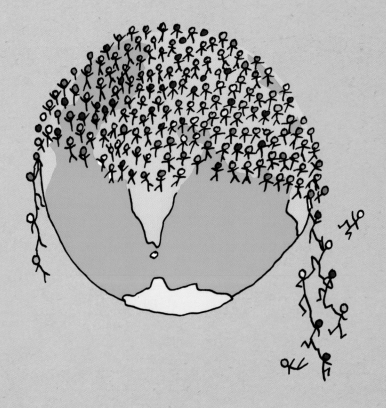

Math uses
numbers to sort
the world.

Contents

About Math

If your eyes glaze over at the mention of math, you're not alone. It can seem a blur of mysterious numbers! But it is one of the cleverest of all human skills, and it can do amazing things. And you use it everyday without even realizing!

What does math do?

Math is a number sorting machine. You put numbers in, juggle them around, and get different numbers out the other end. The way they come out tells you a lot and can give the solution to a very tricky problem. If you want to know how to divide a pizza fairly between friends, math can tell you. If you want to plot your spaceship's course to Mars, math can do that too!

The math families?

Most of the greatest math brains of the last 300 years came from just 24 sets of teachers and their pupils. In the 1700s and 1800s, most math whizzes, such as Friedrich Liebnitz, were German or Dutch. In the last century, the United States was the math superpower.

Katherine Johnson, an inspiring African-American mathematician, whose work was crucial to the first space flights

Math and computers

Without math, there would be no computers. Computers were invented to make solving mathematical problems easier. A special kind of math is used to develop the programs that control math. And computers are now the best way to solve the trickiest mathematical problems.

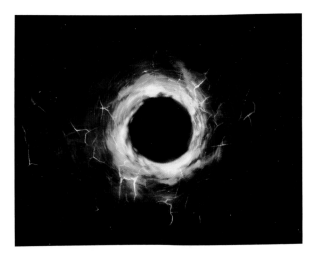

Math and science

Many scientists, especially physicists, are mathematicians too. Math allows you to conduct experiments with things much too big or dangerous to test for real. If you want to know if a black hole could theoretically suck in a planet, math may give the answer. If you want to see how far the explosion from a nuclear bomb will be felt, you can work it out with math.

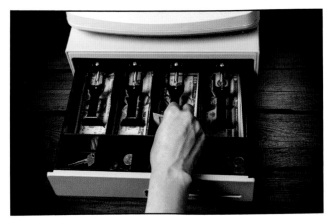

Everyday math

And of course you use it all the time in everyday life. Math tells you if you have been given the right change from a store. It tells you how many days of vacation you have. Or how many points your team needs to avoid coming out at the bottom of the league!

Making It Count

Without numbers, life would be very tricky. You couldn't tell the time. Or know how many brothers and sisters you have. Or how much things cost. Numbers are the basis of mathematics. But where did numbers come from?

Numbers on hand

When people first started to count, they probably used the most handy thing they could find—their fingers. Even before they had the names for numbers, they could simply touch their fingers to count. It's why even today we count in groups of ten—because we have ten fingers.

Making a mark

The problem with finger counting is that there's no way of keeping a record. So about 6,000 years ago, Sumerian farmers began making marks on clay to keep track of things like how many bags of corn they'd sold. The Egyptians developed a clever system for showing larger numbers with pictures called hieroglyphs.

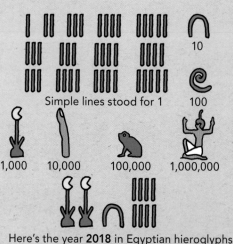

Simple lines stood for 1

10

100

1,000   10,000   100,000   1,000,000

Here's the year **2018** in Egyptian hieroglyphs

X out of ten

The Romans were very methodical people. In the time of the Roman Empire, they set up a regular system of numbers shown by letters called numerals. They are still used today sometimes, such as in the names of kings and queens. The British queen is called Elizabeth II, which means the second.

Here's the year **2018** in Roman numerals: MMXVIII

Numbers one to three are capital "i": I, II, III
5 is V
10 is X
4 is IV and 9 is IX
50 is L
100 is C
500 is D
1000 is M

Knowing your place

The system we use today came originally from India. They had a simple system with just 10 symbols, one for each of the numbers from 1 to 10. Bigger numbers are created simply by adding them in the right place. Each extra place multiplies the number by 10.

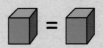

1 one = one

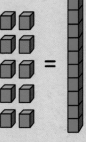

10 ones = 1 ten

The year **2018** in modern numerals means
2 x 1000 . . .0 x 100 . . . 1 x 10 . . . 8 x 1

Big numbers

Big numbers are used both for things that are very big and things that are very small. There is no limit to just how big a number can be. But mathematicians have devised simple shorthands to make very big numbers easier to write down. One is by names for large numbers. The other is by **powers**.

Millions–
population
of New York
(8.5)

Billions–
population
of the world
(7.6)

Trillions–
number of
brain cells (0.1)

Quadrillions–
number of bacillus
that could grow in
one day (16)

Quintillions–
how far away
Andromeda
Galaxy is in miles
(14)

Sextillions–
grains of sand
on the Earth's
beaches

Septillions–
stars in the
universe

Octillions–
mass of the
Earth in
grams (5.98)

Nonillions–
atoms in the
human head
(0.45)

Decillions–
mass of the
sun in grams
(15)

Powers of ten

Another way of writing big numbers is to express them in powers of ten.

- One hundred is ten squared (10 x 10) or ten to the power of two. This is written as 10^2.
- One thousand is ten cubed (10 x 10 x 10) or ten to the power of three. This is written as 10^3.
- Ten thousand is 10 x 10 x 10 x 10 or ten to the power of four. This is written as 10^4.

More or Less

Addition and subtraction are the most basic of all mathematical skills and were practiced long ago in prehistoric times. In fact, it is thought that some animals, including chimpanzees, can perform very simple addition and subtraction.

Adding and taking away

Addition means putting two numbers together to get a third, the sum. It's essentially a process of piling up. Subtraction is the opposite of addition. It involves taking one number away from another to get a third number, the difference.

With addition, you begin with a pile of 3 socks, add 4 more, and count how many socks you have altogether, which is 7 (the sum).

With subtraction, you begin with a pile of 5 socks, take away 2, and count up how many socks you have left, which is 3 (the difference).

Majorities

In democratic countries, many decisions are made by numbers. People vote, and once all the votes are added up, the group or policy with the most votes wins. If you add up all the votes for the winner, then subtract all the other votes, the difference is called the "majority."

In the US Congress, there are 435 members of the House of Representatives and 100 members of the Senate.

Members mostly belong to the Republican Party or the Democratic Party.

● Democrats
● Republicans

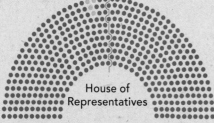

House of Representatives

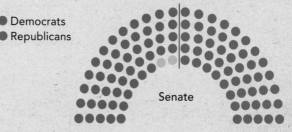

Senate

If the House of Representatives has 238 Republicans and 193 Democrats (plus 4 Independents), the Republicans have a majority of 238 − 197 = 41

If the Senate has 51 Republicans and 47 Democrats (plus 2 Independents), the Republicans have a majority of 51 − 49 = 2

	1	2	3	4	5	6
7	8	9	10	11	12	13
14	15	16	17	18	19	20
21	22	23	24	25	26	27
28	29	30	31			

Take away

For mathematicians, subtraction is the same as addition—except you end up with a "difference," not a sum. The difference is the number you need to add to the subtracted number to give the original number. All computers rely on this way of thinking. Another way of thinking about subtraction is counting backward, as in the countdown to a rocket launch or ticking the days off a calendar.

Winning the league

Sports leagues are simple examples of addition in action. Each team gets a certain number of points for each game, depending on the result—such as 3 for a win, 1 for a draw, and 0 for a loss. Over the season, the points for all their results are added up. The teams are then placed in a league table in order of total points. The one with most points wins.

LA LIGA

	P	W	D	L	F	A	PTS
BARCELONA	36	26	6	4	10	34	84
REAL MADRID	35	26	6	3	96	39	84
ATLETICO	36	22	8	6	66	25	74
SEVILLA	36	20	9	7	63	45	69
VILLARREAL	36	18	9	9	53	32	63
ATHLETIC CLUB	36	19	5	12	51	39	62

Shopkeeper's subtraction

Here's a trick to help with subtracting numbers in your head. It's called the "shopkeeper's method" and works by simple counting. If you wanted to take $8.00 from $17.25, for example, work out what number you add to $8.00 to make $17.25 by simply counting on your fingers or in your head, from 8 up to 17.

How Big

By themselves, numbers don't mean much.
If your friend asks how much money you
have in your pocket, and you say "73," she'd have to say,
"73 what?" Did you mean pennies, dollars, or squirrel's nuts?
So the "what" is important, and mathematicians call this a "unit." With
a unit, the number tells you how many, how much, and how big.

How big?

A unit can be just an object, like a cow. You might
say there are "5 cows" in the field. But a **unit of
measurement** is a standard size that shows how
big something is. Units of measurement could be
length, weight, volume, and many other things.
To record how big you are,
you use units of length, such
as feet and inches or meters
and centimeters.

How tall
are you?

How big is
your head?

How big is
your waist?

How big are
your feet?

How long
are your
arms?

How long
are your
legs?

Why not use a tape measure to take these
measurements and compare them with
your family or friends?

Little and large

Units of length allow us to say who was the tallest
man ever. It was Robert Wadlow (1918–40) of the US.
He was a lofty 8 feet 11.1 inches tall. One meter is
3.28 feet. So he was 2.72 meters tall. Chandra Dangi
(1939–2015) of Nepal was the shortest man ever, at 1
foot 9.5 inches (54.6 cm).

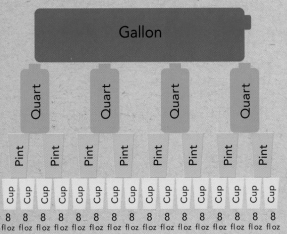

Gallon

Quart Quart Quart Quart

Pint Pint Pint Pint Pint Pint Pint Pint

Cup Cup Cup Cup Cup Cup Cup Cup Cup Cup Cup Cup Cup Cup Cup Cup

8 floz 8 floz 8 floz 8 floz 8 floz 8 floz 8 floz 8 floz 8 floz 8 floz 8 floz 8 floz 8 floz 8 floz 8 floz 8 floz

Setting standards

You can measure things in two main ways: metric and US standard units. In the metric system, units go up in steps of 10 times, 100 times or 1,000 times—for example, 10, 100, or 1,000 millilitres of a liquid. US standard units are more complex and vary according to what you're measuring. Here are the measures for liquids.

Missing Mars

It's really important to know what units of measurement you're using. Three feet is very different from 3 meters. In 1999, NASA's Mars Climate Orbiter space probe burned up in the Martian atmosphere because engineers got their calculations wrong. They had failed to convert from a measurement called US customary units to metric.

Mars Climate Orbiter

Laser for measuring a standard meter

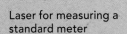

Meter

If things are to be measured accurately in meters, you need to know just how long a meter is. In the past, a meter was the length of a special platinum alloy bar stored safely in Sèvres, France. Now it is set by a laser beam, and is the distance traveled by light in $\frac{1}{299792458}$ second.

Divide and Rule

Multiplying and dividing are two of the key tasks of math. They can sound complicated at first, but they are basically counting in groups. Multiplying is about counting up groups; division is about counting them down.

Multiplying

How many socks will you use in a week if you wear a fresh pair every day? Your group is two socks, a pair. So count or add two socks seven times, once for each day of the week. Mathematicians like to say that's 2 times 7, but it's the same as two 7 times. Every multiplication is the same: you simply add a group a particular number of times. The symbol x means times.

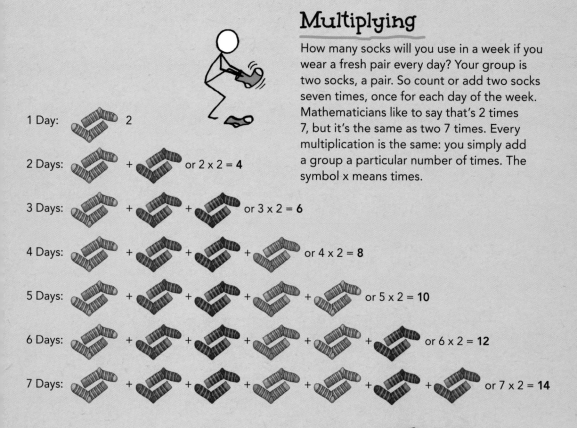

1 Day: 2

2 Days: + or 2 x 2 = **4**

3 Days: + + or 3 x 2 = **6**

4 Days: + + + or 4 x 2 = **8**

5 Days: + + + + or 5 x 2 = **10**

6 Days: + + + + + or 6 x 2 = **12**

7 Days: + + + + + + or 7 x 2 = **14**

Dividing

Dividing is about sharing or counting down. How many days will 14 socks last? Count down or take away two socks (a pair) for each day until you run out of socks.

14 ÷ 2 = **7** or

14 − − − − − − − = 0

Day 1: 12   Day 2: 10   Day 3: 8   Day 4: 6   Day 5: 4   Day 6: 2   Day **7**: 0

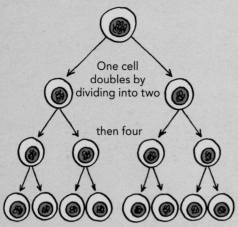

One cell doubles by dividing into two

then four

then eight, and so on . . .

How things grow

Multiplication and division are at the heart of all life. Every living thing, including us, is made of tiny cells. Things grow because these cells are continually splitting in two, or dividing. They grow because by dividing they multiply. One cell divides to become two. Two cells divide to become four. Four cells divide to become eight, and so on. Bacteria do this so quickly that one can become many millions in a few hours. This is how illnesses can spread very fast.

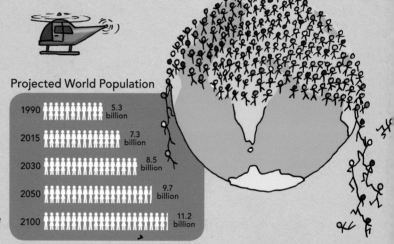

People power

If every mother and father had just two children, the population of the world would stay the same. But many moms and dads have more than two. So the world's population is multiplying rapidly. There are now 7.6 billion people in the world. The population grows by 75 million each year.

Projected World Population

1990	5.3 billion
2015	7.3 billion
2030	8.5 billion
2050	9.7 billion
2100	11.2 billion

On average, children around the world can expect to live 622,000 hours (71 years). Some say the oldest person in the world ever was Li Ching Yuen, who lived 2.24 million hours (256 years). But scientists say that isn't possible.

Dividing time

Time depends on division. Years are divided into 365 days. Days are divided into 24 hours. Hours are divided into 60 minutes. Minutes are divided into 60 seconds. You can see the divisions of the day in hours and minutes clearly on an old-fashioned clock.

Getting the Facts

On their own, numbers mean little. But numbers *of* something is data, which is a useful way of ordering the world. Data is a collection of facts, such as numbers, words, measurements, observations, or just descriptions of things. You can use math to help you collect data and then handle the data you collected.

Elephant facts

If you want to know more about an elephant, you can collect two kinds of data. **Qualitative data** describes something in words. **Quantitative data** is in numbers. You can collect quantitative data either by counting or measuring. Here is some data about elephants. See if you can work out what kind of data each is.

African elephant	Asian elephant
Ears: Larger	Ears: Small, rounded
Trunk tip: Two "fingers"	Trunk tip: One "finger"
Head: Single dome	Head: Twin dome
Height: 9–13 feet	Height: 6.5–9 feet
Weight: 8,800–15,400 lb.	Weight: 6,500–13,200 lb.

Bars and pies

You can simply present your data as lists of numbers, but it's much easier to get the picture if you present it in a graph. **Bar charts** and **pie charts** show the numbers in different groups—bars by the height or length of bars, pie charts by the size of wedge-shaped slices of a pie. Here's a pie chart showing the production and use of oil.

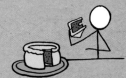

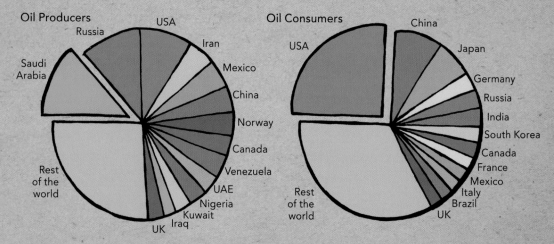

Oil Producers
USA
Russia
Iran
Saudi Arabia
Mexico
China
Norway
Canada
Venezuela
UAE
Rest of the world
Nigeria
Kuwait
Iraq
UK

Oil Consumers
China
USA
Japan
Germany
Russia
India
South Korea
Canada
France
Mexico
Italy
Brazil
Rest of the world
UK

Yellow	IIII	4
Blue	IIII I	5
Red	IIII II	6
Pink	I	1
Green	IIII	4

Making a survey

Surveys are a great way to learn about the world. Some surveys ask people's opinions through questionnaires. Some find out about things, such as how dirty the air is, by taking measurements. Here's how you might find out about the favorite colors of your classmates. There are four steps to every survey (below left).

1 Think up the question or questions. Here, it's "What's your favorite color?"
2 Ask your question. Go around the class asking your question, and record the answers with a mark in the right box.
3 Tally (add up) the results. Add up the totals for each color.
4 Present the results. Make a bar chart in which the height of each bar shows how many like each color.

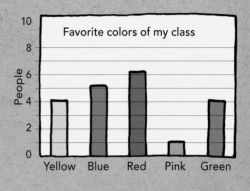

Favorite colors of my class

Line up

Line graphs show the varying relationship between two sets of numbers as a sloping line. It is thought that polar bears are suffering because climate change is damaging their Arctic home. So a zoologist might make a line graph to show the changes in average temperature around the world year by year.

1 Using a ruler, make marks for each year along the bottom, and marks for temperature up the side.
2 Make a dot for the temperature in each year.
3 Draw a line joining up the dots.

Changes in average temperature around the world

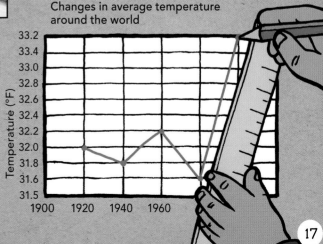

Partial

Every number you can count is called a "whole" number. But there are also partial numbers called fractions. Fractions are what you get when you divide something in an equal number of parts, whether it's pieces of pizza or different weights.

Piece o' pizza

You can think of fractions as slices of pizza. In every fraction, there are two numbers that matter. The **denominator** is how many equal slices you've cut your pizza into. The **numerator** is how many of those slices you've actually got.

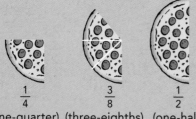

$\frac{1}{4}$ (one-quarter) $\frac{3}{8}$ (three-eighths) $\frac{1}{2}$ (one-half)

When you add up fractions, they can sometimes be made into simpler fractions.

$\frac{4}{8}$ (four-eighths) $\frac{2}{4}$ (two-quarters) $\frac{1}{2}$ (one-half)

When you have more than one piece, you get a mixed fraction

$1\frac{3}{4}$ (one and three-quarters)

You can also put this all as a fraction called an improper fraction.

$\frac{7}{4}$ (seven-quarters)

Numbers compared

In this delicious drink recipe, $\frac{4}{5}$ should always be pineapple juice and $\frac{1}{5}$ orange. But it's much easier to think of these fractions as "parts." You then say the recipe is 4 parts pineapple juice to 1 part orange juice. Here, a part is a glass. It doesn't matter what size the glass is, only that there is always four times as much pineapple as orange.

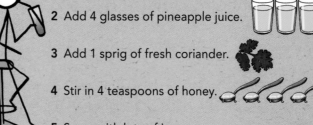

1 Pour 1 glass of orange juice into a jug.

2 Add 4 glasses of pineapple juice.

3 Add 1 sprig of fresh coriander.

4 Stir in 4 teaspoons of honey.

5 Serve with lots of ice.

By the hundred

To compare things, people often use **percentages**. This just means converting every fraction to hundredths—$\frac{3}{4}$ is the same as $\frac{75}{100}$ or 75% (percent). To change a fraction to a percentage, use a calculator to divide the top number by the bottom, then multiply by 100. This chart shows the percentage of people at different ages using glasses.

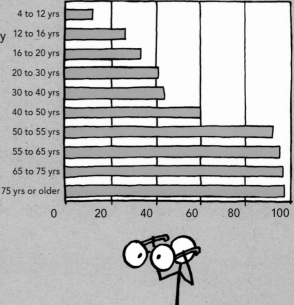

4 to 12 yrs					
12 to 16 yrs					
16 to 20 yrs					
20 to 30 yrs					
30 to 40 yrs					
40 to 50 yrs					
50 to 55 yrs					
55 to 65 yrs					
65 to 75 yrs					
75 yrs or older					

0   20   40   60   80   100

Air mix

Atmospheric gas quantities by volume

Carbon dioxide 0.04%
Argon 0.934%
Oxygen 20.9476%
Nitrogen 78.084%

In any mixture, the proportions of the ingredients are much the same, no matter how much of the mixture you have. The air around us is a mix of gases: oxygen and nitrogen, with small amounts of other gases. In this diagram, the proportion of each gas is shown as blocks out of a hundred. These can be written as percentages (see above).

Are you concentrating?

Most liquids are either acidic or alkaline. When they are very concentrated either way—strongly acid or strongly alkaline—they can be very dangerous, causing severe burns. Their concentration is measured on the pH scale from 1 to 14. A neutral liquid, such as tap water, has a pH of about 7. The strongest acid has a pH of 0; the strongest alkali has a pH of 14.

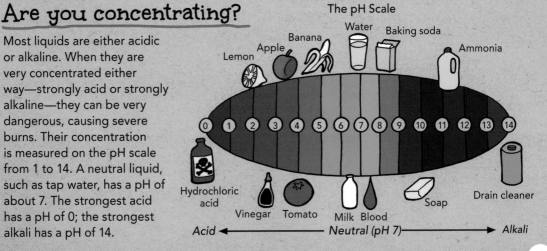

The pH Scale

Lemon Apple Banana Water Baking soda Ammonia

0 1 2 3 4 5 6 7 8 9 10 11 12 13 14

Hydrochloric acid

Vinegar Tomato Milk Blood Soap Drain cleaner

Acid ◄─────────── *Neutral (pH 7)* ──────────► *Alkali*

Getting the Point

Fractions can be fiendishly complicated to work out. That's why decimals are so helpful. The word "decimal" means in tens. Actually, our entire number system is decimal, since it is based on units of ten. But normally when mathematicians talk of decimals, they mean decimal fractions.

Decimating

What decimal fractions do is express every fraction in terms of tenths, hundredths, thousandths, millionths, and so on. And by using a dot called the decimal point after the whole number, fractions can be written as simple digits. A half is five-tenths, or 0.5. A quarter is 25 hundredths, or 0.25. Three quarters is 75 hundredths or 0.75.

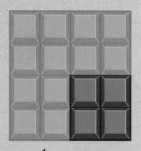
$$\frac{1}{4} = 0.25$$

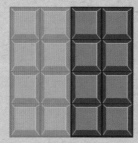
$$\frac{1}{2} = 0.5$$

$$\frac{3}{4} = 0.75$$

There are 100 pence in 1 pound.

There are 100 cents in 1 dollar and 10 cents in a dime.

There are 100 cents in 1 euro.

Working with decimals

The great advantage of decimal fractions is that they can be worked on in exactly the same way as whole numbers. They work especially well for calculators. That's why most money systems today are decimal. There are 100 cents in 1 dollar, for instance, just as there are 100 cents in 1 euro or 100 pence in 1 pound.

Complicated decimals

To change a fraction to a decimal, divide the figure below the line into the figure above. Some fractions are tricky. To work out the **circumference** of a circle, you multiply its radius by a number called "pi," which has the symbol π, and double it. This is written as C = 2πr. Pi is simple as a fraction: $3\frac{1}{7}$. But in decimals it's a number that goes on forever! You can just use 3.142, though. Phew!

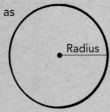

Radius

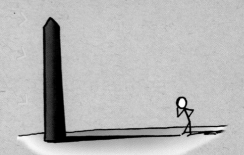

Working out the world

When you're dealing with round things, pi is a big help. Even 2,200 years ago, Greek mathematician Eratosthenes worked out how big Earth is with an ingenious calculation using the shadow cast by a tall tower, the way the sun shined down a deep well, and pi . . .

Just how old

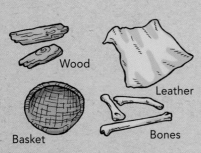

Wood

Leather

Basket

Bones

Archaeologists often measure how old things are by carbon dating. Living things all contain a radioactive chemical called carbon-14. This sends out special energy rays. When things die, the carbon-14 in them breaks down at a steady rate. So you can tell the age of things like the remains of wood and plant fibers from how much carbon-14 they still contain. Decimals make the sums much easier.

100%	50%	25%	12.5%

Age 0	Age 5,730 yrs	Age 11,460 yrs	Age 17,190 yrs

Measuring the breakdown of carbon-14 in a piece of buried wood provides a measurement of the time elapsed since it was living.

Power numbers

The difference in size between an atom and a galaxy is so big we have to write the numbers in shorthand, using powers of ten combined with decimals. Powers are the number of times you multiply a number by itself. One hundred is ten times ten, or ten to the power of two, or 10^2. One thousand is ten times ten times ten, or ten to the power of three, or 10^3. So 1,550,000 is 1.55×10^6.

Fast Work

If you want to see how some things compare, you may need ratios and rates. Ratios will tell you whether there are more girls in your class than normal. Rates will tell you whether you can cycle faster than your friends.

Ratio

A ratio is a relationship between two numbers. If you have 2 red apples and 1 green apple in every bag, the ratio is 2 to 1 or 2:1. You probably know that when you were little, the older you got, the fewer teachers you had to look after you. But you can show this mathematically as a changing ratio.

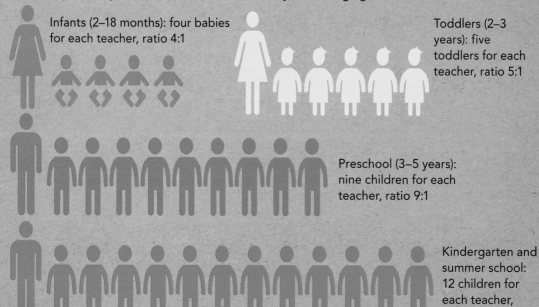

Infants (2–18 months): four babies for each teacher, ratio 4:1

Toddlers (2–3 years): five toddlers for each teacher, ratio 5:1

Preschool (3–5 years): nine children for each teacher, ratio 9:1

Kindergarten and summer school: 12 children for each teacher, ratio 12:1

Heartbeat

A rate is a special kind of ratio. It shows how fast, how many times, or how much something is happening for a particular unit, such as a unit of time or weight. When doctors check your pulse, or heart rate, they are checking how many times your heart beats every minute—usually 60–100 times a minute when you're relaxed.

Getting littler

When you make an accurate drawing, model, or map, you use another special ratio, called "scale." Scale is the ratio of the length or another measure in the drawing to the length in real life. If a model car is a tenth of the length of the real thing, the scale is 1:10.

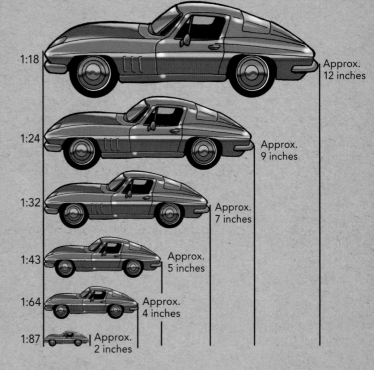

1:18 — Approx. 12 inches

1:24 — Approx. 9 inches

1:32 — Approx. 7 inches

1:43 — Approx. 5 inches

1:64 — Approx. 4 inches

1:87 — Approx. 2 inches

How fast?

Speed is a special kind of rate. It shows the distance traveled in a particular unit of time, typically miles or kilometers per hour or feet or meters per second. An athlete might run 400 meters in a minute. That's the same as 14.9 miles (24 km) per hour, but he almost certainly couldn't keep that pace up for an hour. In his record 100m sprint in 2009, Usain Bolt reached 27.8 mph (44.72 km/h), but for just 20 meters.

Faster and faster

Acceleration shows how quickly something gains speed in a particular unit of time. That means it has the word "per" in it twice. A car might accelerate from a standstill to 60 miles per hour in 10 seconds. So it gains 6 mph in speed in every second, or 6 miles per hour per second. Racing sports cars can accelerate from 0–60 mph in under 3 seconds . . . 1, 2, 3!

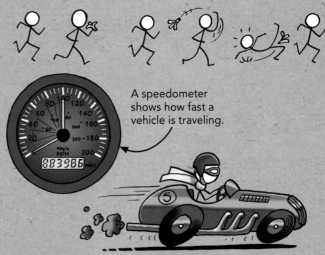

A speedometer shows how fast a vehicle is traveling.

Shaping Up

Angles are the cornerstone of the branch of math called geometry. Whenever two straight lines meet, there is an angle between them. Regular angles are found throughout the natural world—in honeycombs, crystals, and atoms. They are used in the construction of everything from household furniture to massive suspension bridges.

Regular shapes

There are many geometric shapes. They are all made by different combinations of straight lines and curves. They can be either flat shapes that you can draw on paper, such as squares and circles, or solid shapes like spheres (balls), cones, or cylinders. Designers often need to know how much material they'll need to make particular shapes. Here are some shapes and some of the formulas used to work out the areas.

Key: A = area
s = side
w = width
l = length
b = base
h = height
r = radius
d = diameter

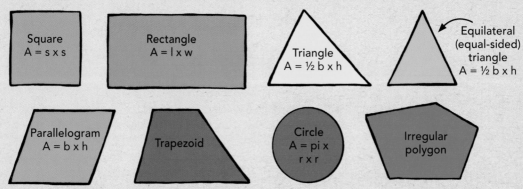

Square
A = s x s

Rectangle
A = l x w

Triangle
A = ½ b x h

Equilateral (equal-sided) triangle
A = ½ b x h

Parallelogram
A = b x h

Trapezoid

Circle
A = pi x r x r

Irregular polygon

How much paint?

Area is the amount of space taken up by a particular flat shape. It's simplest to calculate area for a square, so usually it's measured in units such as square feet or square meters. Area calculations are involved in everything from working out how much material is needed to make a dress to calculating the value of a piece of farmland.

To calculate how much paint you need to paint your bedroom:

1 Measure how long the longest and shortest walls are, and add the two lengths: l + w =

2 Measure or guess the height of the wall: h =

3 Multiply the sum of the wall by 2. So 2 x (l + w) =

4 Multiply your answer by the wall height, to give the area of all four walls. 2 x (l + w) x h = area

The paint shop will tell you how much paint you need to cover the area you worked out.

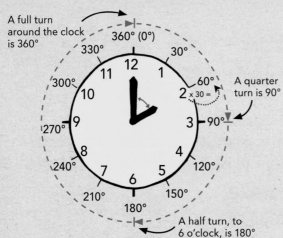

A full turn around the clock is 360°

360° (0°)
330°
300°
270°
240°
210°
180°
150°
120°
90°
60°
30°

x 30 =

A quarter turn is 90°

A half turn, to 6 o'clock, is 180°

Round the clock

Think of angles like the two hands of an old-fashioned clock, with the hour hand stuck on 12. As the minute hand moves, the angle between the two hands gets bigger and bigger. But angles are measured not in hours and minutes but degrees, usually written with the symbol °.

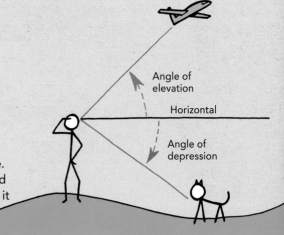

Angle of elevation

Horizontal

Angle of depression

Positive or negative?

An angle can be thought of as the rotation of one line relative to another. If the angle is measured counterclockwise, it is called a positive angle, and if measured clockwise, it is called a negative angle. Similarly, if an angle is measured upward it is called the angle of elevation; if it is measured downward it is called the angle of depression.

What's your angle?

Different names are used to describe different angles and different parts of an angle.

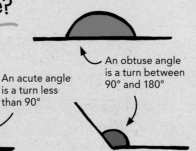

A right angle is when there is a quarter turn, creating a square corner (90°)

An acute angle is a turn less than 90°

An obtuse angle is a turn between 90° and 180°

A reflex angle is a turn between 180° and 360°.

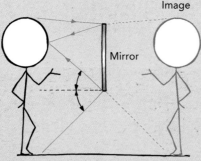

Image

Mirror

How a mirror works—and how to tell if a wall mirror will let you see your feet . . .

Looking acute

You see yourself reflected in a mirror because the light rays hit the mirror and bounce back. They bounce back at the same angle that they hit the mirror, but opposite. You can use this to work out if a wall mirror is long enough to show you all the way down to your feet. The bottom of the mirror—the lowest you can see—must be more than halfway to the floor from your eyes.

Letters Count

In a kind of math called algebra, you work things out by using letters that stand in for unknown numbers. The mystery letters, typically x, y, or z, are known as variables because they can be any number. When mathematicians need to find out what the mystery number is, they put the letter in a special kind of sum called an equation.

Keeping things equal

An equation is a way of saying that two things are equal. So it always has two halves with an equals sign in between. A simple equation might be 2 + 3 = 5. In algebra, 3 might be the unknown number, so the equation would be 2 + x = 5. Your job is to solve the equation to find the mystery number x. Here are some famous equations.

Einstein's famous equation $e = m \times c^2$ revealed the relationship between energy (e) and mass (m).

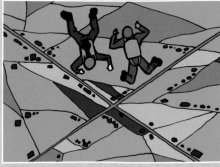

One of Newton's famous equations showed how much gravity makes things accelerate.

Another of Newton's equations was F (Force) = m x a (acceleration), which shows how much force anything moving has.

Pythagoras's theorem $a^2 + b^2 = c^2$ showed how, if you know the length of two sides of a right-angled triangle, you can work out the length of the third side.

Pool power

An algebraic equation is like a pair of weighing scales that must always be balanced. If you do something to one side of the equation, you must do exactly the same to the other side in order to keep it balanced. In this simple problem, you set up 12 balls on a pool table and knock in one after another until you have just 7 left. How many balls did you knock in?

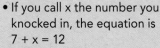

- If you call x the number you knocked in, the equation is
  $7 + x = 12$
- To find what x is equal to, you can take 7 from each side of the equation, keeping it balanced:
  $x = 12 - 7$
- The answer is 5.

Gravity

Vh

Skatepower

Algebra and equations can be used to work out anything from the area of a football field to what electric current you need to make a light glow. They can also be used to understand how different quantities relate to each other, such as how a skateboarder does tricks like the hippie jump. This involves him jumping up and landing back on the board because his speed or "velocity" forward (Vh) matches that of the board.

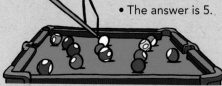

Beginning the universe

Algebra and equations have enabled scientists to work out just how the universe began, even though they can never go back and see for themselves. The math is very complicated, but by adjusting the equations for things we know today, they can wind the clock back to see the forces in play at the dawn of time.

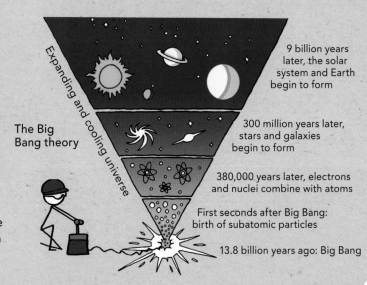

The Big Bang theory

Expanding and cooling universe

9 billion years later, the solar system and Earth begin to form

300 million years later, stars and galaxies begin to form

380,000 years later, electrons and nuclei combine with atoms

First seconds after Big Bang: birth of subatomic particles

13.8 billion years ago: Big Bang

Timeline of Math

Maybe the earliest of all human beings learned to count hundreds of thousands of years ago. But math as we know it today developed in early civilizations—such as the Sumerian, Chinese, and Maya—up to 4,000 years ago. But it was scholars from ancient India, Greece, and Islam who really got the math ball rolling.

1650 BCE

Pi (symbol π) is one of the key numbers in math. We know that the Ancient Egyptians knew pi from a scroll called the Rhind Papyrus. Easy as pi.

300 BCE

Brilliant Ancient Greek scholar Euclid wrote a book called *Elements*, which laid down all the basic methods of geometry (the math of areas and angles) we use now. Getting in shapes.

| 1500 BCE | 1000 BCE | 500 BCE | 0 |

1000 BCE

The Ancient Egyptians were the first to show they could work with fractions. Love them to pieces.

350 CE

Hypatia was the first famous female math whiz. She was Greek and lived in Alexdandria in northern Egypt, where there was the world's most famous university. Girls count.

800 BCE

The Indian mathematician Baudhayana knew all about complicated mathematical methods called quadratic equations. It all adds up.

820 CE

Persian mathematician Al-Khwarizmi introduced algebra to the world in his book *Al-Jabr*, one of the greatest math books ever. Signing up.

1202

Italian math wizard Fibonacci introduced Hindu-Arab numbers to Europe. We still use them around the world. Got his number.

1, 2, 3, 4, 5, 6, 7, 8, 9, 0

1660s and 1670s

English scientist Isaac Newton and German thinker Gottfried Liebniz developed calculus, the math of how things change.

500　　　1000　　　1500　　　2000

1100

Persian mathematician Omar Khayyam found an ingenious way of solving equations and created "analytic geometry," the geometry of graphs. It was later developed by René Descartes. Well coordinated.

1842 CE

Ada Lovelace created a method of calculating and as a result is renowned as being the world's first computer programmer.

1850s onward

Cutting-edge math began to get really complicated!

Puzzlers!

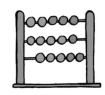

Fermat's teaser

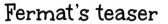

When French math genius Pierre de Fermat
died in 1665, he left a book with an equation
and these words scribbled in the margin:
"I have a truly marvelous demonstration of this
proposition which this margin is too narrow to
contain." For 330 years, countless mathematicians
tried to solve "Fermat's Last Theorem" but failed.
Then in 1995, British mathematician Andrew
Wiles finally came up with the answer!

$$a^n + b^n = c^n$$

Math fight-out

In 16th century Italy, math whizzes fought math duels
to answer tricky problems first. Of course, they kept
their methods secret! Rising star Tartaglia guarded
his solution to one fiendish problem, cubic equations,
so jealously he wouldn't let his publisher Cardano
publish his book. But Cardy pieced it together
from other sources and published anyway. Tarty
challenged Cardy to a duel. Cardy got his secretly
brilliant student Ferrari to fight for him—and
unsuspecting Tarty accepted. Ferrari presented
him with an even more fiendish solution, and
Tarty was utterly humiliated.

Newton vs. Liebnitz

$$E = \frac{M_0 c^2}{\sqrt{1 - \frac{v^2}{c^2}}}$$

It wasn't just the Italians who fought about math!
In the later 1600s, the English genius, Isaac
Newton, and the brilliant German, Gottfried
Liebnitz, got riled up about who invented a new
kind of math called calculus. Their supporters
joined in, sent angry letters back and forth, and
held noisy meetings. It was probably Liebnitz
who got there first. But Newton's ideas were far more
detailed and really set the ball rolling for calculus—
except Newton called it fluxions. Not a great name.

Creasing up

Origami (paper folding) fascinates mathematicians. Until 2002, they were utterly convinced paper could never be folded over more than eight times. Then in January 2002, when American high school student Britney Gallivan was doing a math project, she proved this wrong, folding thin paper 12 times. Britney went on to devise a formula for calculating the length of paper you need to achieve a certain number of folds—and with a clever bit of math, showed 12 is the maximum.

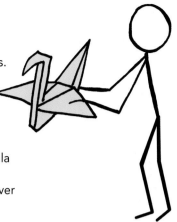

Glossary

algebra: a kind of math that uses letters to stand in for unknown numbers as a way of working things out

bar chart: diagram or graph with bars of varying length or height that shows how much of each group there is

circumference: the distance around the edge of a circle

denominator: the bottom number in a fraction, showing how many parts the whole is divided into

equation: a math expression saying two sets of numbers and symbols are equal

fraction: a part of a whole number, such as a half or a quarter

geometry: the math of shapes, lines, and angles

line graph: a graph that shows the varying relationship between two sets of numbers as a sloping line

numerator: the top number in a fraction, showing how many parts of the whole there are

percentage: the size of something in relation to the whole, described in parts per 100, where 100 is the whole thing

pie chart: a diagram or graph in the shape of a circle or pie, which shows how much of each group there is with slices of varying size

power: how many times to multiply a number by itself

qualitative data: information that describes something in words

quantitative data: information that describes something in numbers, found either by counting or measuring

ratio: the relationship between two numbers showing their relative size

unit of measurement: a standard size that shows how big something is

Index

The Author

John Farndon is Royal Literary Fellow at City & Guilds in London, UK, and the author of a huge number of books for adults and children on science, technology, and history, including such international best-sellers as *Do Not Open* and *Do You Think You're Clever?* He has been shortlisted six times for the Royal Society's Young People's Book Prize for titles such as *How the Earth Works* and *What Happens When?*

The Illustrator

Self-taught comic artist Joe Matthews drew Ivy The Terrible, Ball Boy, and Billy Whizz stories for the Beano before moving on to Tom and Jerry and Baby Looney Tunes comics. He also worked as a storyboard artist on the BBC TV series Bob the Builder. Joe has produced his own *Funny Monsters Comic* and in 2016, published his comic-strip version of the Charles Dickens favorite, *A Christmas Carol*. Joe lives in North Wales, UK, with his wife.

Picture credits

t = top, m = middle, b = bottom, l = left, r = right
Marie-Lan Nguyen – own work, public domain: 28br.
Muhammad ibn Mūsā al-Khwārizmī – John L. Esposito, *The Oxford History of Islam*: 29tl.
NASA/restored by Adam Cuerden: 6bl.
Shutterstock: 4 PM production 7tl; Alones 6tr; Billion Photos 7bl; Christian Bertrand 11mr; FloridaStock 17bl; Georgios Kollidas 29tr; GTS Productions 28bl; itechno 28tr; Jatuporn Chainiramitkul 11bl; poomooq 19m; Rawpixel 19tl; torook 29bl; Vadim Sadovski 7mr.
Wikipedia: 28tl; 29br.
Every effort has been made to trace the copyright holders. And we acknowledge in advance for any unintentional omissions. We would be pleased to insert the appropriate acknowledgment in any subsequent edition of this publication.